Establishing a Federal Judiciary

by

Bruce A. Ragsdale

Director, Federal Judicial History Office
Federal Judicial Center

Federal Judicial Center
Federal Judicial History Office
2007

Contents

Introduction

This module was developed by the Federal Judicial Center to support judges and court staff who want to speak to various groups about the history of an independent federal judiciary in the United States. This module focuses on the establishment of the federal judiciary and the history of the federal court system. Other modules in this series examine the constitutional origins of the judicial branch of government and historical debates on judicial independence. Each module includes four components: an historical overview to serve as talking points; a PowerPoint presentation that can be downloaded to provide a visual guide to the speaker's remarks; a list of suggested discussion questions; and selections from historical documents that can be used in discussion with the audience or incorporated in the speaker's remarks.

Part I.   Establishing a Federal Judiciary—Talking Points

1.   A Federal System

Since its origins in 1789, the nation's court system has embodied the federal character of the government established by the U.S. Constitution. The Supreme Court guaranteed the authority of the Constitution and federal law throughout the nation, while a system of federal trial courts, organized within state borders, reflected the legal traditions of each judicial district and facilitated citizen access to federal justice. The decentralized federal judiciary ensured that individual federal courts had a strong local orientation, while at the same time it united a geographically dispersed nation within a consistent system of federal law. In contrast to most other federal systems of government, the United States preserved parallel systems of federal and state courts, thus further protecting the local orientation of much of the nation's legal affairs.

The federal system of a single Supreme Court and regional trial and appellate courts was the subject of regular reassessment and debate as new states entered the Union and federal jurisdiction encompassed more and more of the nation's legal disputes. For more than a century after the founding of the government, the key debates about the organization of the federal judiciary involved the extension of the court system to new states, the service of Supreme Court justices on lower federal courts, the right of appeal to the Supreme Court, and the balance of state and federal jurisdiction. In the twentieth century, proposals for revisions of the federal court system focused increasingly on the timely processing of growing caseloads and protection of the institutional independence of the judiciary.

2. The Constitutional Outline

Article III of the Constitution, drafted in the summer of 1787, offered only the briefest sketch of the court system for the new nation. The Constitution mandated a Supreme Court, but left for the Congress to decide the size of that court and the schedule for its meetings. The Constitution also granted the Congress the option to establish "such inferior courts" as it saw fit, thus leaving unresolved the delegates' debate on the need for lower federal courts that would assume jurisdiction otherwise exercised by state courts. The constitutional outline for the judicial branch, which stood in contrast to the far more detailed plans for the legislative and executive branches, reflected the delegates' preoccupation with balancing the powers of the elected branches. As part of that system of checks and balances, the Constitution granted the judges of the federal courts tenure during good behavior and protection from salary reductions as a guarantee of some independence from the Congress and the President.

The Constitution offered comparatively greater detail about federal jurisdiction, although it left open the option that state courts might exercise much of that jurisdiction. The "judicial power" of the United States would encompass all cases arising under the Constitution, the laws of the nation, and treaties. It would also extend to admiralty and maritime cases; cases in which the federal government was a party; disputes between states or between citizens of different states; and, until the Eleventh Amendment was ratified in 1795, disputes between a state and a citizen of another state. The Supreme Court had very limited original jurisdiction—over cases involving ambassadors and other foreign officials—but the Constitution granted the high court jurisdiction over appeals of all types of cases involving federal jurisdiction, except as Congress made other provision.

3. Congress and the Judiciary Act of 1789

When the First Congress turned to the organization of the judicial branch, much of the debate centered on whether to establish lower federal courts or to rely on existing state courts to exercise federal jurisdiction. Advocates of a strong central government thought a national system of federal courts was an essential requirement for energetic government. Other members of Congress, recalling the colonial experience under British rule, thought that justice was best served by courts tied to local communities. Those who were suspicious of the concentration of national power wanted to grant state courts authority to hear all cases involving federal law or to limit local federal courts to admiralty and maritime law. The judiciary act approved in September 1789 established a federal court system with broad jurisdiction, but the act reserved a significant role for state courts and guaranteed that the diversity of legal traditions throughout the country would be recognized in the local federal courts.

The Judiciary Act of 1789 established three types of federal courts. The Supreme Court, with a chief justice and five associate justices, would meet twice a year in the nation's capital and hear appeals from lower federal courts and from the state supreme courts. The Supreme Court would also exercise the limited original jurisdiction defined by the Constitution. In each state and in Kentucky and Maine (then parts of other states), a district court with a single judge would have exclusive jurisdiction to hear cases involving admiralty and maritime law and conduct trials of minor federal crimes. The district courts shared with the state courts jurisdiction over small suits brought by the United States.

The most important federal cases would be initiated in the third type of court, called circuit courts, which would convene in the same judicial districts in which the district courts met. The circuit courts had no judges of their own, but were served by two Supreme Court justices and the local district judge. (Congress soon revised the law to require only one justice on each circuit court.) Congress grouped the judicial districts into regional circuits for the purpose of assigning justices to serve on the circuit courts within that region. The circuit courts would hear some appeals from the district courts, but they were primarily trial courts. The circuit courts had exclusive jurisdiction over serious federal crimes and shared with the state courts jurisdiction over suits involving disputes above a certain monetary value, suits involving the U.S. government, and suits between citizens of different states.

Congress protected distinctive state legal traditions by drawing the judicial districts to coincide with state boundaries and by providing for the use of the respective state's rules for most district and circuit court proceedings and for the selection of federal juries. Perhaps most important for protection of regional legal cultures, the assignment of "circuit riding" duties for Supreme Court justices ensured that the judges on the nation's highest court would learn about local legal procedures and would interact with citizens at the point where cases entered the federal judicial system. The Judiciary Act also promoted a local orientation of the lower courts by requiring district judges to live in the district where they served. In response to widespread concerns that defendants in federal trials would be forced to appear in distant courts, the Judiciary Act required civil trials to be held in the district in which a defendant was served with a writ and trials involving the death penalty to be held in the county where the crime occurred.

4.   Partisan Conflicts and the Organization of the Courts

Within ten years of the establishment of the federal judiciary, the organization and jurisdiction of the federal courts became the subjects of fierce battles between the political parties that emerged in the 1790s. In 1801, after several years of debate on reorganization of the courts, the lame-duck Federalist majority in Congress approved an act that created new circuit courts with their own judgeships and greatly expanded federal jurisdiction at the expense of the state courts. The Judiciary Act of 1801 also abolished the circuit-riding duties of the Supreme Court justices. Although the justices had repeatedly asked for relief from circuit duties, the opposition Republicans saw the reorganization of the courts as an attempt by the Federalists to secure their hold on the judiciary soon after they had lost control of the Congress and the presidency. Republicans also feared that the expansion of federal jurisdiction would undermine the state courts and eventually the state governments. Republicans were already suspicious of the federal courts because of what they considered the partisan role of Federalist judges in the prosecution of political enemies under the Sedition Act of 1798.

With the support of President Thomas Jefferson, the new Republican majority in Congress soon repealed the Judiciary Act of 1801 and restored much of the court system, including circuit riding, that had been established in 1789. To Federalists, the repeal and consequent removal of the new circuit judges was a violation of the constitutional protection of judges' tenure during good behavior. The subsequent impeachment of two partisan judges further inflamed Federalist fears, and Jefferson, along with many of his allies, continued to advocate limits on federal jurisdiction and on judicial tenure. The organizational structure of the court system reestablished in 1802, however, would remain the same until after the Civil War.

5.   The Courts in an Expanding Nation

As the population of the United States moved west and new states entered the Union, Congress established additional judicial districts with their own judges. Congress expanded the number of circuits and the number of seats on the Supreme Court—to seven in 1807 and then to nine in 1837—to accommodate the new states and to provide a Supreme Court justice for service on the circuit courts in each of the circuits. Travel was so difficult in some newly admitted states that the district courts temporarily exercised circuit court jurisdiction without a visiting Supreme Court justice, but Congress intended to expand the judicial system defined in 1789 to encompass the entire nation as it grew across the continent, and justices regularly served on the circuit courts in most states in the years before the Civil War.

The growing number of cases before the Supreme Court and the justices' continuing obligations on the circuit courts tested the limits of the judicial system of 1789, and in the second half of the nineteenth century Congress considered various proposals for new types of courts and judgeships. When California entered the Union in 1850, the limits of transcontinental transportation made circuit riding to that state impossible, and Congress created a temporary circuit judgeship to serve California. In 1863, Congress increased the number of Supreme Court justices to ten so that one of them could preside in a Tenth Circuit comprising the far western states. In 1866, Congress restored the number of circuits to nine, and in 1869 established circuit judgeships for each of the circuits. The new circuit judges relieved some of the pressure on Supreme Court justices, who continued to sit on the circuit courts.

6.   Defining Federal Jurisdiction

As the court system expanded with the growing nation, so too did the scope of federal jurisdiction. In the first half of the nineteenth century, the growing reach of the federal government was reflected in new jurisdiction over copyright, land claims, enforcement of the prohibition on the foreign slave trade, and, for a limited time, bankruptcy. As statutes defined more and more federal crimes, Congress in 1842 extended to the district courts concurrent jurisdiction over all federal crimes except those subject to the death penalty. The jurisdiction of the federal courts was also the subject of political controversy, especially as it related to the Supreme Court review of decisions of the state supreme courts. Several state legislatures petitioned Congress to repeal that provision of the Judiciary Act of 1789, but this essential foundation of federal authority over the states remained in place.

The Civil War and Reconstruction led to a substantial extension of federal jurisdiction. The various measures to enhance the authority of the federal courts and limit the reach of state courts culminated in 1875 when Congress granted the U.S. circuit courts jurisdiction to hear all cases arising under the Constitution and federal laws. The 1875 act also allowed parties in a case to remove proceedings from a state court to a federal court whenever a federal question was involved or if parties to the case were from different states.

7.   Circuit Courts and American Political Culture

The practical challenges of circuit riding in a growing nation were so great that proposals to reduce or eliminate the responsibility were repeatedly introduced in Congress, often at the suggestion of the Supreme Court justices, but Congress was unwilling to alter the system. In each recurring debate, representatives and senators warned of the risks of severing the connections between Supreme Court justices and regional trial courts. Congressional supporters of circuit riding predicted that justices who presided only over the Supreme Court in Washington would soon be controlled by a "knot of attorneys" and be merely "paper judges." Daniel Webster, one of the leading lawyers before the Supreme Court as well as a member of Congress, said in a House of Representatives debate that Supreme Court judges would be too isolated to guarantee justice if they did not see in practice the operation and effect of their decisions. As late as 1866, the nation's leading law journal, the *American Law Review*, characterized any bill to eliminate travel to the circuits and duties in the trial courts as a measure calculated "to prevent the Justices of the Supreme Court from ever learning any law." Implicit in these debates were the assumptions that practical law was defined in the regional courts of the federal judiciary and that popular respect for the federal courts depended on the accessibility of justice. Even proponents of eliminating circuit duties spoke of the need to find other ways to make the Supreme Court aware of local jurisprudence, such as requiring geographical representation on the Supreme Court.

8.   Justice Delayed

The expansion of federal jurisdiction, increased caseloads throughout the judiciary, and the responsibilities of circuit riding imposed a tremendous burden on the Supreme Court. By the opening of the fall term of 1890, the Supreme Court faced a docket of more than 1,800 cases. Since the 1840s, Congress had considered a succession of proposals to relieve the burden on the Supreme Court, but the congressional debates revealed the difficulty of balancing a guarantee of reasonably speedy justice with the traditionally broad right to review by the Supreme Court and the popular support for justices' service on the federal trial courts in each state. Initial efforts to restrict appeals to certain types of cases or to disputes involving more than

$5,000 raised concerns about limiting access to justice in the federal courts. Proposals for the reorganization of the courts also had implications for ongoing debates on the balance of federal and state jurisdiction at a time when more and more litigation involved the nation's industrial economy.

Almost all of the proposals for judicial reorganization in the second half of the nineteenth century included some form of appeals court that would have final jurisdiction in designated types of cases. In many bills, the appeals court was composed of all the district judges in a circuit and one Supreme Court justice. Other bills called for the appointment of judges who would sit only on the intermediate appeals courts, and still others proposed that Supreme Court justices, perhaps doubled in number, sit in rotating shifts on regional appeals courts and the Supreme Court. A recurring proposal would have had the Supreme Court itself sit in three panels of three justices to expedite appeals.

9.   A New Type of Federal Court

In 1891, Congress established separate courts of appeals in each of the nine regional circuits and authorized an additional circuit judge for each circuit. The circuit judges would sit with district judges or a Supreme Court justice on three-judge panels in the appeals courts. Certain appeals from the trial courts, including those related to constitutional questions and convictions of capital crimes, would go directly to the Supreme Court, but all others would be heard by the courts of appeals. The decisions of the court of appeals would be final in many cases, including the tremendous number of suits involving citizens of different states, revenue laws, and patent laws, as well as in non-capital criminal convictions. A court of appeals could certify a case to the Supreme Court if the appeals court judges wanted further clarification of a legal question. The Supreme Court could also, through its own discretion and issuance of a writ of certiorari, decide to review and determine a case from the lower courts.

The act of 1891 preserved certain aspects of the old judicial system, such as the circuit courts and the assignment of Supreme Court justices to circuits, although the appellate jurisdiction of the circuit courts was abolished. The chief sponsor of the act, Senator William Evarts of New York, expected that the new appeals courts would reduce backlogs throughout the federal judiciary, thus allowing Supreme Court justices and circuit judges more time to sit in the circuit trial courts. Evarts believed it was still important that the justices and appellate judges "be brought in contact with the profession and the suitors and the people in the courts of first instance as often as possible."

The establishment of the courts of appeals almost immediately contributed to a reduction of the Supreme Court's caseload, but the Supreme Court still faced more cases than the justices could decide within a term. Justices were unable to attend circuit courts regularly, and in 1911 Congress repealed the required circuit duties for justices and abolished the circuit courts, thus making the district courts the sole general jurisdiction trial courts of the federal judiciary. (Justices were still assigned to circuits and were authorized to sit as judges on the courts of appeals.) Most courts of appeals soon had three judges of their own to make up the required panel. To relieve the continuing burden on Supreme Court justices, Congress in 1925 limited to just a few categories of cases the right to review in the Supreme Court. With the justices able to determine most of the cases they would hear, the Supreme Court was able to focus largely on constitutional questions and the settlement of conflicting decisions in the circuit courts of appeals. In 1988, Congress eliminated almost all mandatory appellate jurisdiction of the Supreme Court.

10.   The Modern Federal Judiciary

The most notable changes in the federal court system over the twentieth century were those of scale. Congress divided existing circuits to create a Tenth Circuit in 1929 and an Eleventh Circuit in 1980. The District of Columbia circuit gained a court of appeals in 1893, and by the mid-twentieth century, Congress, through a series of acts, granted that court the same status as the other courts of appeals. In 1982, Congress established the U.S. Court of Appeals for the Federal Circuit with jurisdiction over special categories of cases, including patent law and international trade. Many states were further divided to establish additional judicial districts, and the district courts were served by multiple judges. The number of district judges increased from 67 in 1900 to 212 in 1950 and 678 in 2006.

In the second half of the twentieth century, caseloads increased at a rate far greater than population growth. The increase in federal litigation had many sources, including new federal regulation, the enactment of more federal rights, the federalization of crimes formerly prosecuted in state courts, and a greater reliance on federal courts for private suits. New kinds of judgeships helped to expedite this growing business of the courts. In 1968, Congress established the position of magistrates, later called magistrate judges, to replace the commissioners who had long helped to process cases before the formal beginning of trials. Magistrate judges have since assumed greater responsibility for pretrial proceedings and the trial of some misdemeanors. In 1978, Congress established a formal position of bankruptcy judge, replacing the referees who had assumed judicial duties in addition to their administrative responsibility for bankruptcy cases. The bankruptcy judges serve as a unit of the district courts and preside over almost all bankruptcy proceedings. In the second half of the twentieth century, the number of court staff also grew to meet the administrative demands of increased caseloads.

Over the course of the twentieth century, Congress provided the judiciary with its own independent administrative bodies. The Conference of Senior Circuit Judges, established in 1922 (now called the Judicial Conference of the United States), provided the judiciary with a panel of judges who advised Congress on needed legislation and later became the courts' governing board in administrative matters. The Administrative Office of the U.S. Courts, established in 1939, provides the judiciary with the administrative support that formerly came from departments in the executive branch. The Federal Judicial Center, established in 1967, provides education for judges and court staff and conducts research on improving case management and judicial administration.

11.   An Enduring Federalism

The three-tiered structure of courts established in 1891 continues to define the federal judiciary, and the decentralized system of district courts established in 1789 preserves the federal character of the court system—the unique mixture of the national and the local—as envisioned by the founding generation. The history of the federal judiciary suggests that it will always be subject to debates on the most effective organization of individual courts and circuits and on the proper extent of federal jurisdiction. As it has throughout its history, however, the federal judiciary will likely continue to represent a balance between the principle of a consistent and authoritative body of federal law and a commitment to a court system accessible to citizens in every part of the nation.

Part II.   Establishing a Federal Judiciary—Suggested Discussion Topics

1. The Constitution authorizes Congress to establish lower federal courts, but it does not require any federal court other than the Supreme Court. Why did members of the first Congress establish federal district and circuit courts?

    Related Documents: 1, 2; Related Talking Points: 2, 3, 7.

2. For more than 100 years, Congress required Supreme Court justices to serve on federal trial courts throughout the nation, despite the enormous practical difficulties of travel and of managing the growing caseload in all federal courts. What was the role of the justices in the trial courts? Why were members of Congress so determined to preserve the circuit responsibilities of the Supreme Court justices?

    Related Documents: 3, 4, 5, 8; Related Talking Points: 3, 5, 7, 8, 9.

3. Since 1891, Congress and the courts have steadily restricted the right to review by the Supreme Court until that court's jurisdiction is now almost entirely discretionary. How has this restriction on the right to review changed the role of the Supreme Court within the system of federal courts?

    Related Documents: 3, 6, 9; Related Talking Points: 9.

4. How has the federal court system reflected and protected different legal traditions and procedures throughout the nation?

    Related Documents: 1, 3, 5; Related Talking Points: 1, 3, 7.

5. The Bill of Rights guarantees a "speedy" trial in criminal prosecutions, and Senator Joseph Norton Dolph and Chief Justice William Howard Taft believed speed and efficiency in all court proceedings were essential to maintaining public confidence in the judiciary. Why did Dolph and Taft think efficiency was so important in the court system? Did their emphasis on speed and efficiency conflict with other traditional goals of the federal judiciary?

    Related Documents: 7, 9; Related Talking Points: 8, 9, 10.

6. The dual state and federal court systems have made the judiciary of the United States nearly unique among nations with federal governments. Why did the supporters of the Judiciary Act of 1789 propose to divide jurisdiction over some types of cases and to authorize shared jurisdiction in other types of cases? How

has the balance of federal and state jurisdiction changed over the course of United States history?

Related Documents: 1, 2, 6; Related Talking Points: 1, 2, 3, 5, 6.

Part III. Establishing a Federal Judiciary—Historical Documents

Note: The text and descriptions of many of the statutes establishing the structure of the federal judiciary are available on the Federal Judicial Center website (http://www.fjc.gov/history/home.nsf) at "Landmark Judicial Legislation."

Debates on the Judiciary Act of 1789

1. Representative James Jackson of Georgia, in support of a motion to omit district courts from the plan for the federal judiciary, August 29, 1789.

The Constitution does not absolutely require inferior jurisdictions: It says, that "the judicial power of the United States shall be vested in one supreme court, and in such inferior courts as the Congress may from time to time ordain and establish." The word may is not positive, and it remains with Congress to determine what inferior jurisdictions are necessary, and what they will ordain and establish, for if they chuse, or think no inferior jurisdictions necessary, there is no obligation to establish them. It then remains with the Legislature of the Union to examine the necessity or expediency of those courts only. Sir, on the subject of expediency, I for my part, cannot see it, for I am of opinion that the State courts will answer every judiciary purpose. . . .

I hold that the harmony of the people, their liberties and properties will be more secure under the legal paths of their ancestors, under their modes of trial, and known methods of decision. They have heretofore been accustomed to receive justice at their own doors in a simple form. The system before the house has a round of courts, appellate from one to the other, and the poor man that is engaged with a rich opponent, will be harassed in the most cruel manner, and although the sum be limited for appeals, yet, Sir, the poor individual may have a legal right to a sum superior to that limitation, say above a certain amount of dollars, and not possess fortune sufficient to carry on his law suit: He must sink under the oppression of his richer neighbor. I am clearly of opinion that the people would much rather have but one appeal, and which in my opinion would answer every purpose: I mean from the State courts, immediately to the supreme court of the continent.

[Document Source: *Documentary History of the First Federal Congress*, vol. 11, Debates in the House of Representatives, First Session: June–September 1789. Eds., Bickford, Bowling, and Veit. Baltimore: Johns Hopkins University Press, 1992. 1353–54.]

2. Representative Fisher Ames of Massachusetts, in opposition to a motion to omit district courts from the plan for a federal judiciary, August 29, 1789.

A government which may make, but not enforce laws, cannot last long, nor do much good. By this power too, the people are gainers. The administration of justice is the very performance of the social bargain on the part of government. It is the reward of their toils—the equivalent for what they surrender. They have to plant, to water, to manure the tree, and this is the fruit of it. The argument therefore, *a priori*, is strong against the motion, for while it weakens the government it defrauds the people. We live in a time of innovation; but until miracles shall become more common than ordinary events; and surprize us less than the usual course of nature, I shall think it a wonderful felicity of invention to propose the expedient of hiring out our judicial power, and employing courts not amenable to our laws, instead of instituting them ourselves as the constitution requires. We might as properly negociate and assign over our legislative as our judicial power; and it is not more strange to get the laws made *for* this body than after their passage to get them interpreted and executed by those, whom we do not appoint, and cannot controul.

[Document Source: *Documentary History of the First Federal Congress*, vol. 11, Debates in the House of Representatives, First Session: June–September 1789. Eds., Bickford, Bowling, and Veit. Baltimore: Johns Hopkins University Press, 1992. 1356–57.]

Debates on the Repeal of the Judiciary Act of 1801

3. Senator Abraham Baldwin of Georgia, in favor of repeal of the Judiciary Act of 1801 and the restoration of circuit duties for Supreme Court justices, January 15, 1802.

In taking a general look at the two systems, the strongest point of distinction which seizes the first view, is, that in the old system the same judges hold the Supreme Court here, and a court in each of the States, with the exception of the States over the mountains; in the new system, now proposed to be repealed, this is not the case; the courts in the several States are held by different judges. This had ever appeared to him a radical and vital failure in the new system; it deprives judges of the opportunity of a full knowledge of local laws and usages, and destroys the possibility of uniformity; it is also a main artery of healthful circulation in the body politic. In giving a satisfactory administration of a Government over a country of this vast extent, the great object must be to avoid the necessity of dragging the people from the remote extremes, the distance of thousands of miles, to the seat of our Government, or far from their homes, where they cannot have the usual advantages in courts of justice. While two of the judges of the Supreme Court held a court in each State, this was almost entirely avoided, except in some of the largest States. The suits were rarely determined at the first court; at the second court, the judges were considered as bringing the sense of the Supreme Court on the subject; it seemed to give as satisfactory a conclusion to the business as if the parties had been themselves before the Supreme Court.

[Document Source: 7th Cong., 1st sess., Jan. 15, 1802, *Annals of Congress*, vol. 11, 102–03.]

4. Representative John Stanly of North Carolina, in opposition to the repeal of the Judiciary Act of 1801, February 18, 1802.

Under the former system, there were six judges of the Supreme Court of the United States, who held two sessions of the Supreme Court in each year, at the seat of Government. Those judges also held in each State a circuit court, two terms in each year. . . . From the errors of this system resulted, first, a delay of justice. The judges bound to hold courts in succession at remote parts of the continent, were continually travelling; from the variety of accidents to which travellers are subjected in this country, from the condition of roads and overflowing of rivers, it frequently happened that the judges failed in their attempts to get to the courts, or arrived so late that little business was done. Suitors, jurors, and witnesses, were subjected to the trouble and expense of attending courts without the accomplishment of their business; hence resulted a delay of justice. . . .

Another great evil resulting from that system was, its tendency to lessen the character and respectability of the Federal bench. Those best acquainted with the profession of the law will most readily admit, that even a life of patient study is unequal to the complete attainment of principles and rules; and that much labor and industry are necessary to preserve that which is gained. Consequently, that extent of legal knowledge, correctness of judgment, and respectability of character, which should designate the persons qualified for this important trust were seldom to be found, but in men far advanced in years. Men possessing these qualifications, not inured to labor, are seldom equal to the fatigue of their duty; or, if at the time of appointment, fast approaching to the infirmities of age, were not to be expected to relinquish the enjoyments of private life for an office, which, however honorable, subjected them to the fatigue of a day laborer. The office, with its incumbrances, was, as it were, offered to the lowest bidder. And men best qualified to honor the bench, were driven from it.

[Document Source: 7th Cong., 1st sess., Feb. 18, 1802, *Annals of Congress*, vol. 11, 569–70.]

Debates on Circuit Riding

5. Representative Daniel Webster of Massachusetts, in defense of the circuit duties of Supreme Court justices, January 4, 1826.

In the first place, it appears to me that such an intercourse as the Judges of the Supreme Court are enabled to have with the Profession, and with the People, in their respective Circuits, is itself an object of no inconsiderable importance. It naturally inspires respect and confidence, and it communicates and reciprocates information through all the branches of the Judicial Department. This leads to a harmony of opinion and of action. The Supreme Court is, itself, in some measure, insulated; it has not frequent occasions of contact with the community. The Bar that attends it is neither numerous, nor regular in its attendance. The gentlemen who appear before it, in the character of counsel, come for the occasion, and depart with the occasion. The Profession is occupied mainly in the objects which engage it in its own domestic forums; it belongs to the States; and their tribunals furnish its constant and principal theatre. If the Judges of the Supreme Court, therefore, are wholly withdrawn from the Circuits, it appears to me there is danger of leaving them without the means of useful intercourse with other Judicial characters, with the Profession of which they are members, and with the public. But, without pursuing these general reflections, I would say, in the second place, that I think it useful that Judges should see in practice the operation and effect of their own decisions. This will prevent theory from running too far, or refining too much.

[Document Source: 19th Cong., 1st sess., Jan. 4, 1826, *Register of Debates*, vol. 2, 877–78.]

Debates on the Establishment of Courts of Appeals

6. Views of the Minority, U.S. Senate Committee on the Judiciary, August 8, 1890.

It is not perceived by the undersigned upon what principle it is that all cases in which the jurisdiction of the national courts is invoked by citizens of different States, aliens, etc., are excluded from review by the Supreme Court. The Constitution puts suits of that character upon the same footing as suits drawing in question the Constitution of the United States and the laws of Congress—as being entitled to the same judicial consideration of the national authority as the others, and for very obvious reasons. The judicial establishment of the United States was created for the purpose of defending and enforcing all rights (and in an equal degree) existing under the national character of the Union; and it was thought, undoubtedly, that among the most important of these was that of protecting a citizen of one

State against any local bias that might exist against him in another and distant community.

This, we think was and is even more important than the consideration by a national court of subjects arising in respect of the construction and effect of the Constitution or of a national law; for, in the absence of any local bias, it may be justly supposed that the local court, whether State or national, would be likely to decide such questions impartially, and on the whole correctly; while in the case of local bias, it may, at least to a certain extent, just as well exist in a national court administering the laws in a particular community, as in a State court. We believe, therefore, that the Supreme Court ought to have jurisdiction to review cases arising in the national courts in the various States when their jurisdiction has been invoked on the ground of citizenship or alienage quite as much as in cases where the jurisdiction is not thus invoked, but depends upon the construction of the Constitution or a law.

We are compelled to think, therefore, that the attempt made in the scheme of the majority of the committee to diminish the number of causes coming to the Supreme Court is, in the respect before referred to, arbitrary, and not defensible upon any consideration other than the necessity of finding some means for a more rapid disposition of causes in that court. We believe it to be important to the best interests of the whole people in every part of the Republic that every suitor in the courts of the United States should have an equal right to take the judgment of the highest court of the Union upon his particular case, be it great or small. If there be an overruling necessity to limit the jurisdiction of the Supreme Court in order that justice may be finally and speedily administered, of course that necessity must be yielded to and provision made accordingly. But we think that the Supreme Court may, without excluding from its consideration any case that now by law may be brought to it, dispose speedily of all causes that may be upon its calendar from year to year, without any exclusion of any class of cases of which it now has appellate jurisdiction. We think this can be done, as in one form or another it is done in the States and in other countries, by providing that the Supreme Court shall hear causes coming to its appellate jurisdiction by acting in separate divisions of three or more justices, and, thus going on with three hearings at the same time.

[Document Source: Senate Judiciary Committee, Views of the Minority, 51st Cong., 1st sess., 1890, S. Rep. 1571, 2–3.]

7. Remarks of Senator Joseph Norton Dolph of Oregon, September 19, 1890.

To force a litigant into the Federal courts to-day to await the long-delayed decision of the court of last resort is equivalent to a denial of justice. What is the plain, imperative duty of Congress in the premises? It is to provide adequate judicial machinery for the prompt transaction of the business of the Federal courts. If this is not done, these courts, instead of answering the great and beneficial purpose of their creation and affording speedy and impartial justice to litigants, will become, if they have not already become, by reason of the inadequacy of the judicial system and the long delay to which litigants are subjected, instruments of oppression and wrong, the means of denying justice to meritorious litigants in many instances forced into them for the purpose of delay.

[Document Source: 51st Cong., 1st sess., Sept. 19, 1890, *Congressional Record*, vol. 21, pt. 10, 10227.]

8.   Remarks of Senator William Evarts of New York, September 19, 1890.

I have heard it said by persons in great authority that under this scheme, after this accumulation is once worked off, as we hope it may be by some extraordinary effort on the part of the court so as to bring about practically the benefits, a session of five months here might dispose of the docket, and that therefore these justices might be liberated for doing a share of judiciary duty in the courts of the first instance.

I do not know whether all the Senators will agree, but for myself I regard it as a great misfortune that judges in banc are also not brought in contact with the profession and the suitors and the people in the courts of first instance as frequently as possible. Now, I will imagine—for perhaps I can not call it more than imagination—that these circuit judges, who are to compose this tribunal in each of the circuit courts in their appellate function, will, as I think, be able to dispose of the annual litigation in three or four months, at such distribution of terms as they may think fit, and they would be left to take the very important part that they now take, and can not be spared, in my judgment, in the court of first instance in equity cases and in matters that belong to first hearings of all important matters.

I do not desire to see a severance between these appellate judges, which the scheme of the House operates between the judges of that court and the jurisdiction in the first instance of the litigation that the circuit judges now discharge.

[Document Source: 51st Cong., 1st sess., Sept. 19, 1890, *Congressional Record*, vol. 21, pt. 10, 10222.]

Administrative Reform of the Judiciary

9. Chief Justice William Howard Taft's Recommended Changes in Judicial Administration, Address to the Chicago Bar Association, 1921.

The three reforms, therefore, to which I invite your attention are, first, an increase in the judicial force in the trial Federal courts, and an organization and effective distribution of the force by a council of judges; second, simplicity of procedure in the trial Federal courts; and, third, a reduction in the obligatory jurisdiction of the Supreme Court and an increase in the field of its discretionary jurisdiction by certiorari. It thus will remain the supreme revisory tribunal, but will be given sufficient control of the number and character of the cases which come before it, to enable it to remain the one Supreme Court and to keep up with its work. I venture to ask the members of the Bar of the United States and of this important Bar to aid the cause of justice by promoting the legislation which I have attempted to describe.

There is no field of governmental action so important to the people as our courts, and there is nothing in those courts so essential to the doing of justice as the prompt dispatch of business and the elimination from procedure of such requirements as will defeat the ends of justice through technicality and delay. While the Bar and the Bench are really much less responsible for delays in legal procedure than the public are likely to think, the very fact that they are popularly supposed to be responsible should make us act with energy to justify the existence of our profession and the maintenance of courts.

[Document Source: William Howard Taft, "Three Needed Steps of Progress," *American Bar Association Journal* 8 (January 1922): 34–36.]

Bibliography

Felix Frankfurter and James M. Landis. *The Business of the Supreme Court: A Study in the Federal Judicial System.* 1928. Reprint, New Brunswick, N.J.: Transaction Publishers, 2007.

Russell Wheeler and Cynthia Harrison. *Creating the Federal Judicial System.* 3d ed. Washington: Federal Judicial Center, 2005.

History of the Federal Judiciary. Federal Judicial Center website. http://www.fjc.gov/history/home.nsf